Stunt Man

by Stephen Rickard

Published by Ransom Publishing Ltd.
51 Southgate Street, Winchester, Hampshire SO23 9EH
www.ransom.co.uk

ISBN   978 184167 784 2

First published in 2010

All photographs copyright © 2009 - inside front cover, pages 16/17, 18, 19 -
Rob Friedman; title page, pages 20/21 - TRanger; page 5 - chang; pages 6/7 -
Chris Rogers; pages 8/9 - Christophe Michot; pages 10/11 - Jeannot Olivet;
pages 12/13, inside back cover - Lars Christensen; pages 14, 15 - Majoros
Laszlo; page 22 - Karen Williamson; page 23 - Chanyut Sribua-rawd.
All other photographs courtesy Adam Kirley.

Many thanks to Adam for all his help.

A CIP catalogue record of this book is available from the British Library.

Stunt Man

STEPHEN RICHARD

Ransom

You'll find me in the movies.

But you won't know it's me.

PROD.

ROLL	SCENE	TAKE

DIRECTOR

CAMERA

DATE   DAY NIGHT INT EXT MOS

I do the dangerous stuff. But I always pretend to be another actor.

Sometimes we do stuff like diving or jumping from high places.

We must do everything that the film needs and that is too dangerous for the actors to do.

And we never take a risk.

We plan everything so that we are in control.

Stunt people train for years. We learn all the tricks from older guys.

So **never**, *never*, try a stunt yourself.

For fire stunts we must plan well.

Nothing must be left to chance.

He has a face mask and breathing equipment, too.

But firemen must put out the flames after about two minutes.

It gets too hot.

Any longer and the stunt man would get burned.

The biggest risk is that you might breathe in fire or hot smoke.

It can burn your throat and lungs.

I was a stunt man on the James Bond film *Casino Royale*.

This is the stunt crew for the film.

I was stunt man for Daniel Craig.

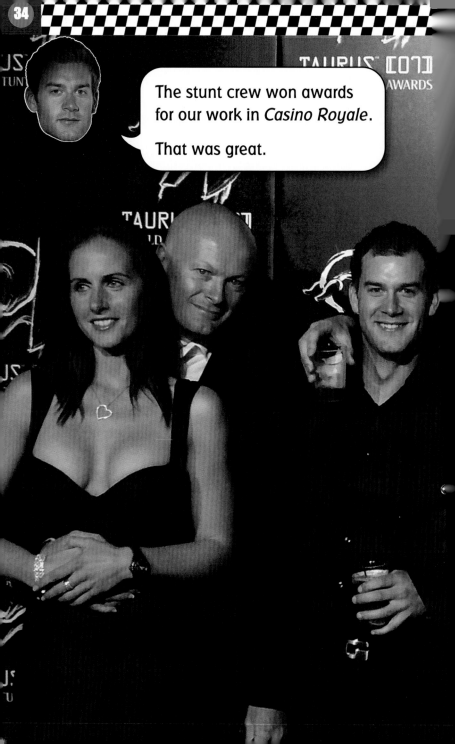

Jargon Buster

actor
Aston Martin DB9
breathing equipment
Casino Royale
control
dangerous

full body burn
mistake
risk
stunt
stunt crew